# The Hermit
## Lucy Ives

The Song Cave

Published by The Song Cave
www.the-song-cave.com
© 2016 Lucy Ives
Design and layout by Mary Austin Speaker
Cover image © Iwajla Klinke, Untitled, from the series
*Bescherkinder*, 2010

ISBN 978-0-9967786-3-3
Library of Congress Control Number: 2016938905

FIRST EDITION

# The Hermit

*This is the etymological situation of Alice, who
learns from the White Knight that the name of
a song is called "Haddock's Eyes," the name
is really "The Aged Aged Man," the song is
called "Ways and Means," and the song really
is "A-Sitting on a Gate."*

SUSAN STEWART, *NONSENSE*

1.

A man claims he makes a choice to be unhappy, since it allows him vigilance. "I am vigilant and suffering," he tells us. And perhaps this is the very anatomy of unhappiness: a choice to engage in a certain perception, which is to say, *experience*.

2.

In a notebook, in a strange list of place names: "Mushroom Town"

Mallarmé appears to me in a dream as two women. Clutching the back of a nearby chair, a blue pigeon chortles, bows.

## 3.

Desire counterfeits time, is the voice of narration, of narrative (= promised emancipation). I write, inconclusively, "All culminating in the image of a dwelling: It indicates a secret life. Since all of writing is devoted to the question of unremembered pleasure..."

4.

Because the question is, generally, what it may mean that this is happening (to someone)—while, for a certain woman I know, it remains, peculiarly, a question of *what* is happening, by which I mean, what or which thing (indeed, which life) "it" is.

5.

Title as autobiography: Hazlitt, *My First Acquaintance with Poetry*

Title as autobiography: Coleridge, *The Friend*

## 6.

The relationship of plot to text is productive but not direct. This suggests an additional reason for the intactness of the novel through modernism, its formal evasion.

I stopped writing for years and instead had ideas. I talked with people. How to make an idea small or large enough that it not become an interruption or intrusion, I asked. (Within a novel, for example.)

A strange point, yet possibly true: America, lacking a great urban novelist, had been too influenced by philosophy.

7.

I depend on others to provide me with material. *As when Nietzsche*, etc. What if we, like Bacon ("wonder is broken knowledge"), think of the aphorism as a sympathetic form? Yet I'm unable to separate sympathy from commiseration, i.e., improved despair.

## 8.

A man, still young at this point in the story, considers how
he senses desire in others. He has thought of it as his own
possession, their desire, and this has led him to behave stupidly.
One is implicated but not automatically, not without one's own
permission, for there is no good in love. One loves actively,
on principle—or one attempts, erroneously, to possess desire,
as he has done. And yet, the young man thinks, it is no better
not to love. It seems like truth to him; it takes the form of a
command. He grows old. He is old. He is old and alone, but
still thinking. He wants to know what would constitute a true
command. Is love a command? The man may even be dying
now, is about to die, is dying, when he begins to ask himself, Is
it not my own permission that lends love this form?

9.

On a country road, I pass an abandoned sign:

      THO    AS         TRY  CLUB

Rebecca says, "This is a poem about trying to write a novel."

## 10.

Publication is a fiction. It contributes to the reality of sentences that otherwise have no real being. The act of publishing establishes as a reality, too, the fiction of a reader, whether or not anyone reads.

## 11.

"I" is a small cut. Whatever is on the other side of presentation (the object that is this book, this page) enters through it, into relation. The book's aspirations to be real are, nevertheless, stronger than mine. "I" is an example. Every text cannot be said to have a narrator.

12.

Someone says, "Charm plays a certain role in getting someone to trust you."

A pair of assignments discovered in a notebook from 2001: *A. List of various lives, written as directives or recipes (now do this, now…) B. A several-pages-long play in which many hundreds of characters speak only once*

13.

Houellebecq: Paradoxes are elegantly dramatized, as if the author had been, in a sense, gagged. Unable to generate commentary of any kind, he portrays events "in themselves."

The "bait" of recognition.

14.

I find a stanza:

> I had cake in my ears like
> We were washing each other's ears
> Like this cake smells so good
> This was we were 19
> Now I never write
> I see things in the air more
> I mean I see things in the air
> More frequently

## 15.

What if a person will always be a few steps from life, whatever this is, and what if this person will feel dissatisfied, imperfect on account of this distance? What will we say of them? Do they become a character typical of their time? And, if such a person cannot become such a character, what is the use of them?

A phrase recurs: "the triumph of real sympathy"

I want to write an essay about the novel as a site of novelty, where the proposition "Anything can happen" is somehow tested.

16.

Vox quae non scribi potest: vox illiterata. (*A voice that is unable to write: an illiterate voice.*)

Would happiness be a gift, were it to make itself known? A proof of weakness?

From a list of books to read: Virginie Despentes, *Baise-moi, King-kong Théorie*; Susan C. Boyle, *From Witches to Crack Moms*

## 17.

On Sunday, after our interview, sitting with Sam, there isn't a quality of being *with* him, rather only of being with oneself (of being oneself) in his presence.

18.

Oppen: "He sees in the manner of poetry."

Realism as ellipsis.

## 19.

Necessity of finding an area in which one is not an impartial actor. Necessity of finding an area in which one desires the living of others.

20.

Like Kathy Acker, I wanted to write a letter to Heathcliff at a certain point in *Wuthering Heights*. But I wanted to speak to him over the phone.

In a notebook I discover an exceedingly general series of statements (yet they seem to form the sum of my education): *One technique was to begin with a principle. What was desired was for something to come into existence. This created entity would circulate in books. The entity was not necessarily or exactly a fiction, since it could not* remain *a fiction—since productive of fame, livelihood, etc.*

Out of fear I have perhaps done a poor job of recording my own thoughts. I look away from the page. I am not even looking at the page. I am still not looking.

21.

Perhaps this can be a poem about how I think about the future.
It can be a poem of servile innocence. Since I do not "think"
about the future.

22.

I read through my journals, 2010 to 2014. In summary: many lists; I get caught up in petty disputes; do not know what I in fact am, since the "knowing" I desire is something like "real being." Must think more softly, in the face of modernism.

23.


He says to me, before I speak, "Can you look at me as like one of the smartest women in the world, because that's what you are? <u>Look</u> <u>at</u> <u>me</u>."

24.

Zachary talks about wanting to be with someone because he feels like he can be a better person for someone else. He says he doesn't know what he's doing, wishes he had someone to do things for. I tell him I think we are very different people.

Theory as pure verbalism: a generated knowledge with negative impact.

If I begin to miss someone, I think, "Life is bad anyway."

25.

Someone imagines herself as a weak outlier of modernism.

There are parts of reading ("aspects") that remain unnamed.

Lyotard: "*L'utopie est que la vérité ne paraît jamais là où elle est attendue.*" (Below this phrase, in a notebook, multiple versions of the sentence in English indicate excited reading. Here I display only the most literal, "Utopia is [the fact?] that truth never appears where it is expected.")

26.

A hut is a small house.

27.

I liked that (as you put it) "fairly relentless pursuit of a particular kind of past."

It's possible that the novel becomes necessary (to a writer) when one perceives and cannot simply "think through" others, personalities. One enters into a circular relation, in attempting to solve contingency, something not even productive of lyric. Thus the novel could be the elaboration of nearly real situations as an aid, a kind of paradoxical recovery from the actual.

Impulse of some novelists: fear, pessimism, a hatred that finds no relief in reality.

28.

Fragment suddenly recalled from a conversation in a dream: "You know I'm the kind of person who just thinks symmetrical faces are the most beautiful," as she imagines (joyfully) a symmetrical face.

29.

"I thought of you" means: "What I said to myself; a variety of sentences I could remember others saying."

An Argentine professor watches an American student take notes. Regarding the form of her presence, he remarks, "She draws a line."

Someone traffics in her youth.

30.

The pitiful nearness of what does come to pass and, therefore, incessantly replaces that which we intend as our existence.

Locations are eccentric. Here and now. Not the movement of "closer"; rather, "otherwise."

A phrase in a notebook: "Dickinson as anti-Bovary"

The worst is my imagination: lushly underscoring everything.

31.

You cannot win. This was what she feared, in its possibly
perfect truth. You cannot win. There are no "winners."

A woman in a story is overheard saying, "Whatever happens,
it has either already happened or has always been about to
happen. This has been true since the day we met."

32.

Fragment: "Tries to kill sorrow with vanity"

## 33.

I wake from a dream in which Charles Olson is smothering me
with his inner thigh. He stands over me, presses his semi-erect
penis, under the material of his chinos, against my cheek and
eye. There is a sweet smell, as of detergent.

To experiment with every kind of prose imaginable, e.g., the
proses of America. I ask, What is the purpose of clarity, beyond
description? Clarity, but to what end? The exquisite prose of
Melville, of—what is totally different and yet feels related—
Rousseau.

34.

Lines from a magazine: "LES ANNÉES DIX? THE NINETIES HAVEN'T HAPPENED YET"

35.

The worst is my imagination.


A note: "Must begin studies of description."

36.

Yesterday fielding a question from Jay, something about why do I not write about affect, reply that for me the only affect is—or affect is only—an expression of the wish "Let me not be destroyed."

I remember the precision with which I experienced time when young. I am only saying this since there is almost nothing that can restore this precision, this specificity, except arousal.

I can't describe myself as a poet. I'm the author of some kind of thinking about writing.

37.

That a kind of experiential or "in-the-world" engagement should impinge on how a canon is taught. Nearby these notes now, on the same page, a fragment has appeared: "*que les étudiants ont décidé d'abandoner, joyeusement, leur passé*"

From a list of texts to read: Susan Howe, "Statement for the New Poetics Colloquium, Vancouver. 1985"

38.

An argument

1. We are supposed to use elements, aspects, of daily life to interpret art (which is therefore different, separate, from so-called daily life).
2. A novel is composed of versions and/or aspects of daily life.
3. Could we use art to interpret daily life? (E.g., a conversation with my mom can be explained by a painting by Ken Okiishi?)
4. The structure of plot is one thing. The structure of the work of art—another.
5. A novel: In which plot is "replaced" by the work of art. In which art "interprets" life.
6. Of a painting. Of a sculpture. This is what I mean. I do not mean there is one universal structure. Bear with me. I'm asking you to make generalizations that could prove useful, as in, in the future.

39.

Possible for me to write 200 words in a day, any day, every day. Thus, 73,000 words per year. At 250 words per day, I write 91,250 words per year.

40.

Notion: Elaborate, extended descriptions of scenes in *A Nightmare on Elm Street* in which Freddy does not appear.

41.


Imagine that love between two people is of such parity that
one has only to hear the other speak; then, in an instant,
remembers years of kindness. Why won't the other speak now?
Why does he seem to become lost, as if inside his own living?

42.

An essay occurs in time like dog years, where it isn't a task of reasoning so much as something that befalls one. I perhaps don't read or write enough and yet always feel like I am reading, like I am writing.

43.

One must work, perhaps for some time, to see scenes.

44.


A conversation recorded now nearly a decade ago:

*What is something exquisite?*
A snake is.
*A snake. Why is a snake exquisite?*
No. The human.
*Why is a human exquisite?*
Because he has two of everything, two eyes, two hands, two feet.

45.

An artist tells me, "The writing is the, um, 'human term' in this."

I say, "So, you like looking at failure."

46.

Affection, attraction, compulsiveness, compulsively picking, picking at a scab, squeezing a puppy, pity, wrenching vanity...

47.

Cutting into a view: the relentlessness of representation (some
kind of essay on collage). Attempting to "see" the way in
which the eye cuts out.

Dream last night about a museum in Queens called either
LOUIS or LOUY—or, now that I think of it, LOUIY. (The
spelling won't become certain.) It is on the edge of land,
perhaps over an ocean, though I do not remember seeing ocean
while there; it is an old, small castle, something like a folly.
Inside, harmony with the name: textiles, a kind of pattern,
iteration, smallness, intensity; something I associate with the
1980s as an intellectual zone, if ever it was one. Gold light
and a field of sand and gravel separate the folly from some
larger, longer armory-like structure, probably constructed
at the beginning of the twentieth century, in which the
administration must be housed. Everything conscientiously
restored. Whitewash. I think I am with my mother. Later, at
what might be J.'s house. I remain open to all that is said to me
by people who are 24. Also, somewhere in the dream S. crying
softly, a conversation about my "percentages."

49.

50.

Why is it that nature may possess immanence (may be said to), but the citizen, not? In other words, a storm that destroys one's house is violent; the desire to protect one's house merely quantitative, social?

I get (i.e., comprehend) "the conceptual"; yet, what I desire most is the writing of a great contemporary philosopher.

Christine on literary realism: This is when coincidence and personal connections (interrelatedness) drive a story (are a story?), e.g., "It turns out that everyone actually knows one another"; "So-and-so turns out to *actually* be related to another person, instead of just present in or at the same place and time."

A fragment: "*Orphée, symbole de l'amant-poète*"

## 51.

At the end of her unfinished novel, a strange art object appears:

On a folding table buckling under great weight sat a cube-shaped structure of 4' x 4' x 4'. It was constructed from dark wood, the exterior worked with carvings of figures in relief: a parade of animals. Each animal imitated, to the best of its abilities, the carriage of a human, starting with the cat, who balanced a stick at the end of her nose, upon which stick balanced a lemon. Behind followed a goose, behind the goose a spaniel, behind the spaniel a sheep, behind the sheep a monkey, a goat, a wolf, a cow, a horse, a bear. The wolf was playing a clarinet or long pipe, and thus the other animals all appeared to be in the midst of a dance, each kicking out one curly-haired paw or hoof in a kind of coordinated ecstasy. They processed along a hillside that overlooked an ocean. Clouds hung from the rear wall of the carving and in the distance sat a mountainous island with a pair of brick fortresses atop it; a cliffy peninsula, with breakers foaming at its base. This vertiginous mass returned the eye to the mainland of the foreground, where at the center of a plain sat a series of columned arches, betokening a single-storied hall. From the keystone at the center of each arch there hung a ribbon tied in an elaborate knot, and from this ribbon hung a bunch of myrtle, along with the symbol of some trade or craft; one saw a pair of crossed keys, a ship's anchor, a scythe, an hourglass, a drawing compass, a beehive, a spade, a bridle, an anvil, a lyre, a harpoon, a scale, an ear of wheat, a whip, a hammer, a rifle. In a field beyond this hall, littered with curving wildflowers, there ran a pack of hounds, and these hounds were joined by two male figures on horseback, one of whom held both his hands to his mouth as if to amplify a voice, and all ran in pursuit of a stag, who leaped over a stile before a thick woods, in the narrow young trees of which perched a round-eyed owl and a pair of spotted pheasants. In a clearing stood three more stags; at the right and left these animals leaped in profile and at center the third stag stood on a pile of rocks; shoots of leaves sprung from the ground beneath his hooves. Fruit trees, apple and pear, grew in an orchard beyond this scene, and then came vast expanses of cultivated land, lines of tilling like grooves left by the teeth of a comb. A clear stream reflected in its surface the small bodies of a passing flock of sparrows; and a group of rabbits, basking in the grass alongside these waters, were overseen by a boy with a switch in one hand and a ball in another, who wore a strange brimless hat. The sky was shot with veering doves. On one long, rocky slope were a series of ancient crosses, each of which was bowed with age and from which tresses of parasitic plants dangled. A hermit in a peaked hood picked his way among these grim reminders of human law and folly. Before the hermit jogged a horse. Below the man and animal, one saw a valley. Within this valley were ruins of a brick villa with a domed roof. Giant flowers, rose and geranium, grew from vases, and on the front of each vase was the face of a bearded sea sprite or almond-eyed dryad. A spring arranged itself into a natural fountain just beyond this architecture. Water shot in curling symmetrical jets...

## 52.

I discover that writing, as a profession, is about putting oneself into a constrained position, from which there are limited means of escape. The undertaking is not about the words themselves or even some technical skill distinct from survival. One must possess only the ability to tolerate a given position long enough to make it intelligible to others.

## 53.

When I was 13 I swore to myself that I would become a novelist.

54.

I have always wished to recover from a certain amnesia. It is not exactly my own (does not represent a "loss" in my "personality"), nor is it the same thing as forgetting.

Just as purchased goods can never "turn around" to bestow value on the currency that has communicated them…

55.

A poem:

> In the garden, the words bowed their heads;
> They folded in half, moved
> As if I had thrown something from my hand
> To the base of the illuminated column,
> And it caught there and disappeared below the surface
> Like a coin fed back into the earth.

56.

I wanted to write the story of a metamorphosis. The story
is at least partly based on a dream I recall from the diary of
another writer. In the dream, which may not be a dream but
simply a vision the writer has while seated at his desk, an
image of a white horse appears on the wall. It is a white horse
that haunts the writer's mind. The white horse has escaped
its traces somewhere on an urban street. It is moving toward
the suburbs with an eye to the countryside. It is successful in
this movement because it progresses without hurry. It does
not gallop. It moves along the street with the gait of a horse
that drags a heavy cart behind it. The horse moves successfully
toward its liberation since it does not appear to be a fugitive.
My heart beats more quickly when I think about this story,
which I have almost certainly partially invented. The horse
hides its fear of slaughter. It plays a game.


Irony is a kind of secrecy. It is a principle of groups.

57.

If someone fears me, I may think, "At least I am a woman."

58.

A dream: A night goes on for years. One must make use of public transportation in order to cross it. Then: discomfort of daybreak, though perhaps over the course of months; fatigue of brightness.

59.

You tell yourself it is a desire to fade, to walk backward into scenery. This is the general way in which you despair about friendships.

In movies there is no such thing as "experience" for the professional—who is, therefore, a *type*—only necessity, skills.

I find a fragment written on an index card: *"rescues" address by converting it into allegory = author as hero*

From a list of books to read: Mustapha Khayati, *De la misère en milieu étudiant*

## 60.

*A game*: Imagines a past version of herself and compares present iteration to this—or, rather, present self is paraded before past self for judgment. Past self has powers of speech and imagination. Present self is, interestingly, too preoccupied with own current problems to give much shrift to past. Present self extremely difficult to speak to; in fact, taciturn, keeps looking in the wrong direction.

61.


*A game*: Makes hundreds of lists. No titles on lists, each simply starts with an item. Every item must be the most interesting thing the writer can conceive of. And so begins: a monumental failure…


"The life! The life!" a character is yelling.


Just an abstraction, for example, of something that may or may not have happened in the past: I think about other people. No, I press myself against them. I ask myself, can I learn? I think about others.

62.

When I was young or fairly young, I only remember being unable to stop committing errors.

Zachary says, "You have an OK marriage." I want to say, "You have an OK idea of what is interesting."

"It's some wish of another I remember. Or don't remember and continue not to remember. I start to remember and continue not to. No, it's a dead state." (She experiences desire.)

63.

"It's antithetical. You say none of our aesthetic or moral judgments are accurate, meanwhile I render 'none' as plural (an impossibility!). Because nothing exists except the whole, and the world does not have an instinct for self-preservation." (She steels herself against doubt.)

A sentence changes midsentence.

64.

List for Lorine:

     a.   abstraction
     b.   light + shade
     c.   italics
     d.   serifs
     e.   "
     f.   and many times
     g.   '   '   '   '
     h.   I've seen it there

65.

Part of what makes a given movement "memorable" is its being
(having been) collapsed into one. The explicit rejection of
universality on the part of certain actors. And yet: There is a public.

The rhetoric of THERE IT IS upon which: all critical
engagement depends (a constitutive act of description). Trying to
imagine the outside of a given project, its surrounds, cajoling...

Another list:

    a.  Evidence from reading, as well as changes in pitch
    b.  Word as unit
    c.  *Drive*
    d.  "whereas when you read certain
    e.  combinations come out at you"
    f.  Retraction of statement
    g.  How not to take just one path
    h.  Oh, I would certainly say a kind of purgatory...
    i.  July 4, 1983
    j.  following years of health problems
    k.  amphetamine use and an avid addiction to diet pills"

66.

New list:

a. Highly contextual
b. Actual looking
c. Smelling
d. Tasting
e. "without you"
f. From previous experience
g. Could be firsthand, though not obtained through
h. senses, ha
i. "you," "always," "unless," "repeatedly"
j. So not "always"
k. Should appear about to
l. It does not look like it will stop raining
m. Consequence
n. LSD
o. Discussion of the pale
p. Place!
q. Beyond which, "infernal dogmatism"

67.

America is a way of doing things.



Make an illogical jump—dissociation—but, then, imperceptibly—so, quickly—return to render it logical before anyone has seen. In this way, you may seem to improve on reason.

Dream of Denmark. A beautiful but potentially dangerous fog covers the ground; white along the top, periwinkel ether core. A bar we consider as a meeting spot for a subsequent day is named "estiman"—written out with additional spacing, "e s t i m a n." There is an editor with me, tall, blond, uninteresting. Is the D. we meet "the real D."? I have to give him shopping bags made of woven translucent plastic. He puts these in a "European" backpack. I have a car.

When awake I Google "estiman" and put it into an anagram generator. (For the latter, two results I like: "names it" and "means it.") And in Spanish it is a verb: second-person or third-person plural, "esteem, consider, deem." Looking again at this sentence: *A bar we consider as a meeting spot for a subsequent day is named "estiman"—written out, "e s t i m a n."* It could be rewritten: "A bar we consider as a meeting spot for a subsequent day is named '*they consider*'...'*t h e y c o n s i d e r.*'" And does this mean that things are as they appear? The land was covered yet things have names; recognizable actions occur and can be remembered.

69.

He told me that they had conversations about that poet's openness—these are his words, not mine—in which one of them would propose a line or phrase exemplary for its stupidity, and the other would defend these words.

I remember I used to spend months and almost years in dreams, or what are perhaps better termed recollections. I wrote constantly. This was what it seemed appropriate to do. And later: I spent many years with a strong, almost violent feeling that there was much to live for, although I may have been inactive for much of this time.

70.

There have to be some essays that reflect on what can be seen in a glance. It's necessary to have these essays because I can't think of any other way of posing my question, which is to say: Is there that which can *only* be seen in a glance?

I wanted to be present for myself. I would say, "to." But that is not the right preposition.

There are seven gunshots as the sun is setting.

71.

Travel is an aid to memory.


To read: Rémy de Gourmont, *Esthétique*

72.

When, in your book, are you going to get around to talking about the things that, a., are not permitted and, b., will therefore never happen?

*Catalogue:* Images perceived in sleep; images perceived with eyes shut (waking); images perceived in light...

(An anachronistic democratic gaze, apparently forgotten since the 1930s.)

73.

Irigaray: "Their properties are our exile."

74.

I recall now someone saying, "You are both strong-willed people." Is this a description of what happened, or is it a description of something else?

## 75.

Even with geographic proximity, there may exist temporal systems such that two people cannot meet one another or will never meet again.

Dream last night includes swimming. Something about a thick river, keep riding boats on it, travel from station to station, temporary home to home. It is Berlin or a group of islands called "Connecticut." I am alone or have a child or am with my brother. It is sunset, when one seeks something.

Is it possible we somehow die for a time, a year, a month, a day, without realizing this, then awake to find ourselves, which is to say "someone," present again, attentive, expectant, apologetic even?

76.

You may think, "I will always feel like this." You may think, "I cannot change quickly enough," or: "I cannot change 'correctly.'"

## 77.

I thought also, last night, as I resolved to stop reading and get back to work, that I have always done one thing, which is to think to myself, "There is another world, and when at last we are in this other world, all the parts that currently do not touch, in this world, will touch, in that one, and all the ways that I feel, in this world, either will have reality or will have been resolved, in that one." The thought is so familiar that it is mostly unclear, challenging to articulate, a mush. What is the other world? And why is it—having had this thought last night, today, as I once again seek to write it down, having several times promised myself that I would write it down—impossible to reformulate? I can't seem to represent or know the thought again, so entirely familiar.

A white home, mint mansard, ivy browning on a trellis. Shade in foreground. Branches pendant with parasitic vines. Now we are inside. A tan mother is here in a navy blazer. She pours vodka from a frosted bottle into a tumbler near her cereal bowl. She has been eating while standing.

On TV: footage of a slaughtered body. A gurney bears it away.

A teenage girl approaches from the stairs. She wears pale pink. She's sickening in her youth, mouth an overripe strawberry and big, plain teeth.

The mother's hand, with costume jewelry, slaps the TV off. The mother draws her shoulders together. She doesn't want the girl to leave.

The girl holds an orange backpack.

The mother pecks the girl's cheek, her fingers on her daughter's face.

It's very bright and now on the street the girl walks with a blue purse and orange backpack.

Before a Spanish colonial garage she pauses. Across the street is a man in sunglasses and a suit. Is he an agent of the law? The girl looks away, then back, but the man is gone. Breeze tousles things. The girl, staring, is seized from behind by a dark-haired boy. He drags her down an embankment hitherto imperceptible. "You were screaming like crazy," the girl says. "The door was locked from your side," she tells him.

A police officer appears. He holds a long black pistol. There is a chase. The boy is cornered by squad cars and subdued. The girl retreats. The officer with the pistol is her father.

Now we are in English class. There is floating yellow and/or turquoise light. Maps are everywhere. The girl is here. Someone stands at the front of the class and reads with a fat tongue. Now the murder victim in her translucent duffel beckons, and black liquid is in a pool. Human blood so plentiful that it is black. (I saw a sight like this on the floor of the subway once, years before I met you.) Quote: "I could be bounded in a nutshell and count myself a king of infinite space, were it not that I have bad dreams."

79.

Description is just a series of tricks about recognition?

80.

The present as a time we visit.

A is denial. B is self-preservation.

I do not know for how long any of the characters in this book can persist as characters.

# Notes

Literal translations of two phrases in French follow: "that the students joyously decided to abandon their past"; "Orpheus, symbol of the poet-as-lover" (a phrase from the notebooks of Paul Valéry).

The cover image is by photographer Iwajla Klinke, from her series *Bescherkinder*.

The image in entry 49 I found by chance. It is a fairly exact picture of the administrative building of the museum, "called either LOUIS or LOUY—or, now that I think of it, LOUIY," of the dream described in entry 48.

The title of the book bears some explanation. Of course, in entry 51, a hermit appears. But this is only a hermit in a work of art. I'm not sure, at any rate, what a hermit is today.

Strangely, the hermit I have in mind is most closely or accurately figured by the character Nancy Thompson, as portrayed by actor Heather Langenkamp, in *A Nightmare on Elm Street*. Why is Nancy a hermit? Because she is entirely isolated from others, though she is by no means distant from them.

Nancy is secluded in a place of psychological horror and physical violence. Sleep (acquiescence) presents a constant threat. It is Nancy's unspoken decision, a brave one, to believe in the reality of this seclusion, in the ineluctable threat of Freddy's choice to appear to her, that ultimately preserves her life. "He's dead, honey, because Mommy killed him," Nancy's mother maintains. Although I don't like this character very much, I understand what she is saying. See also, entry 78.

Excerpts from this series appeared in *BOMB, Company, Faultline, New American Writing, New Madrid,* and the anthologies *February* and *Some Pigeons Are More Equal Than Others.* Thank you to the editors for their interest and friendship.

Thanks, too, to Sam Frank for his notes on this manuscript.

# OTHER TITLES FROM THE SONG CAVE